W9-CHR-501

Careers in Robot Technology

Joshua Gregory

Published in the United States of America by
Cherry Lake Publishing, Ann Arbor, Michigan
www.cherrylakepublishing.com

Reading Adviser: Marla Conn, MS, Ed., Literacy specialist, Read-Ability, Inc.

Photo Credits: Cover, science photo; page 4 (left), eHrach; Page 4 (right), Riksa Prayogi; page 6, Beros919; page 8, vectorfusionart; page 10, Andrey Suslov; page 12, Gordenkoff; page 14, DuxX; page 16, Betastock; page 18, Africa Studio; page 20, Olesia Bilkei; page 22, YAKOBCHUK VIACHESLAV; page 24, Phovoir; page 26, Zapp2Photo; page 28, Suwin. Source: Shutterstock

Library of Congress Cataloging-in-Publication Data

CIP data has been filed and is available at catalog.loc.gov.

Printed in the United States of America.

Table of Contents

Hello, Emerging Tech Careers!

In the past ...

Groundbreaking inventions made life easier in many ways.

In the present ...

New technologies are changing the world in mind-boggling ways.

The future is yours to imagine!

WHAT COMES NEXT?

Who would have thought?

Alexander Graham Bell invented the first telephone in 1876. In 1879, Thomas Edison invented the first electric lightbulb. The Wright brothers successfully flew the first airplane in 1903. And don't forget Henry Ford! He invented a way to make cars quicker and cheaper.

These brilliant inventors did things that people once thought were impossible. To go from candles to electricity? From horse-drawn carriages to automobiles and airplanes? Wow!

The sky's the limit!

Now technology is being used to do even more amazing things! Take **robots**, for instance. Robots are machines that are programmed to do two kinds of things. Some robots do things that people can't do like lift really heavy objects. Other robots are designed to do things that humans don't want to do like vacuum floors. Who knows? Someday there may be robots that can help you clean your room!

This book explores the people and professions behind robots. Some of these careers, like robot technician, are so cutting-edge that they didn't exist just a decade or so ago. Others, like programming, offer exciting new twists using robots.

Read on to explore exciting possibilities for your future!

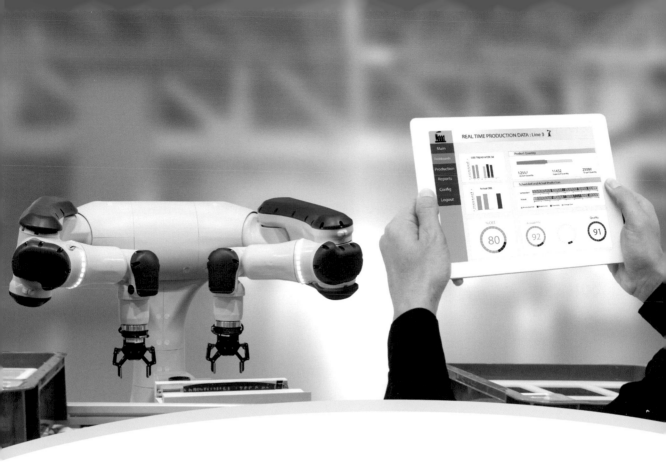

Artificial Intelligence Scientist

"Hi," says the robot, turning its head to look you in the eye. "It's nice to meet you," it continues as it reaches out to shake your hand. As you return the handshake, you are amazed at how much the robot acts just like a real person.

Today's robots are getting smarter and smarter. They aren't humans, but they can do many of the things people can. Some are able to carry on basic conversations with people. They can even detect human emotions and respond with appropriate facial expressions. Robots like this have been employed as tour guides and receptionists in some parts of the world.

These kinds of robots, and countless others, rely on something called artificial intelligence, or AI for short. AI is powered by computer programs. These programs allow robots to "think" and make complex decisions. For example, AI-driven cars are able to safely navigate busy streets without causing traffic accidents.

Scientists and engineers have been thinking about AI and studying its possibilities since the first computers were invented in the mid-20th century. The term *artificial intelligence* was first used by researcher John McCarthy in

Imagine It!

➡ A big part of a scientist's job is to identify problems and look for solutions.

➡ Think about times you've used AI programs before. Some examples include Apple's Siri and Amazon's Alexa.

➡ Make a list of the ways you think these AI programs could be improved.

Dig Deeper!

✅ Watch two AI-powered robots learn to move around and speak to each other: http://bit.ly/TalkRobots.

Artificial intelligence scientists program robots to think and act in human-like ways.

1955. At the time, the most complex AI programs could solve math problems and play board games such as checkers.

Today's AI programs are far more complex. They are used to do everything from predicting the weather to controlling the movements of enemies in your favorite video games. But as impressive as AI technology has become, we still have a lot to learn. This is where AI scientists come in. These forward-thinking experts conduct experiments to try and push AI technology forward.

One day, AI scientists hope to create computers that are able to think for themselves just as well as humans can. However, they still have a lot of work to do before this dream becomes a reality!

Future AI Scientist

AI research is a fast-growing field with plenty of future opportunities. Working as a high-tech scientist generally requires an advanced degree in an appropriate subject, such as computer science or engineering. However, that doesn't mean you can't start learning and researching right now. Read up on basic computer programming skills, and always stay up-to-date with the latest AI news online.

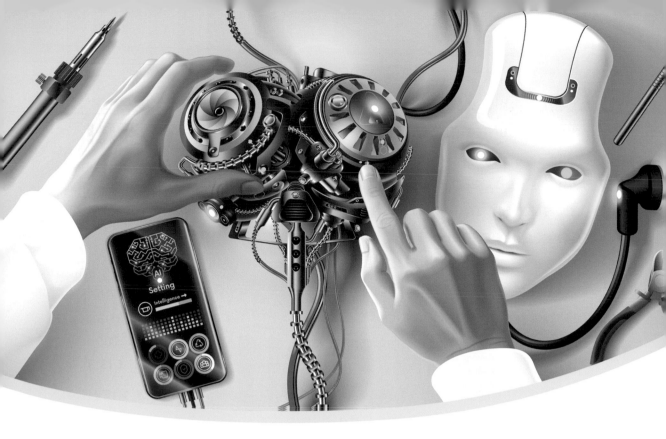

Materials Engineer

You can't believe how much it seems like you are shaking a real person's hand. You know the robot's skin is made of plastic, but it is just as soft as the real thing. The robot's hand even has lines and wrinkles like the ones on your own hands. How did the robot's creators do that?

Robots are highly complex machines. Each one is built from countless smaller parts. For example, a robot built to look somewhat like a person might have a metal "**skeleton**" inside. Its outer covering might be made of plastic. Inside are wires, circuit boards, and other electronic devices. A variety of sensors allow the robot to gather information about its surroundings.

When engineers are building new robots, they don't simply piece together any objects they can find. They think hard about the different **components** that will make up the robot. Each piece has an effect on the robot's ability to function correctly.

For example, robot designers might know that they want to form a plastic shell for their robot's outer covering. But what kind of plastic will they use? There are many different varieties, and new types are still being invented. Some are hard and strong, but easy to crack.

Imagine It!

→ Imagine you are building a new robot. Should it be made of metal or plastic?

→ Make a chart comparing the pros and cons of the two materials. For example, metal is very strong, but it is also heavy.

→ Now think about what you'd like your robot to do. Which material would work better for this kind of robot?

Dig Deeper!

✔ Watch a video showing how engineers and artists use a variety of materials to build lifelike robotic dinosaurs: http://bit.ly/RobotDino.

What a robot is made of helps determine what a robot can do.

Others are softer, but more flexible. Different plastics feel different to the touch. Some are more likely to melt under high heat. These are all things that can affect how well the robot works.

Robot builders often rely on the **expertise** of materials engineers when they are designing the parts for their robots. Materials engineers perform experiments on plastics, metals, and other raw materials. Sometimes they try to find out whether a certain material will function correctly under specific conditions. Can it bear enough weight? Can it be formed into the correct shape for its intended purpose? Will it get too hot when the robot is in use? Depending on their findings, they might need to improve the material in some way. Or they may have to try to create a brand-new material to meet the needs of a cutting-edge robot design.

Future Materials Engineer

Like most jobs dealing with robot technology, materials engineers generally need to have a college degree. You'll need a strong knowledge of physics, chemistry, and math. You'll also need experience conducting experiments in a laboratory. Get started on the path to becoming a materials engineer by doing simple science experiments at home or at school.

Mechanical Engineer

What comes to mind when you think about robots? Do you think of the futuristic characters in your favorite science-fiction movies or video games? You might be surprised to find robots in your own home! Many of the latest vacuum cleaners, lawn mowers, and other household devices are robots.

So, what is a robot, exactly? It is pretty much any type of machine that can move around and do things on its own. The word *robot* was first used in the early 1900s by a playwright named Karel Čapek. It comes from the Czech word *robota*, which can mean "hard work" or "slave labor." Čapek first used the term in a play about machines that people built to do work for them.

Today, there are robots all around us. There are robots that help build things, such as those used to assemble cars in factories. There are robots that help people explore dangerous or far-off places, such as distant planets or the insides of volcanoes. Some robots can create artwork, and others are simply fun toys to play with.

A robot can have almost any shape you can imagine. Some are enormous machines. Others look a lot like people. Some are incredibly tiny! A robot's size and shape all depend on what it was built to do.

Imagine It!

→ Sketch out some ideas for a new robot design.

→ What is the robot's purpose? What features will it have?

→ Label the parts on your drawing.

→ Try building a prototype of your robot. You can use Lego bricks, craft supplies, or anything else you have on hand.

Dig Deeper!

✔ Robot technology is always changing and improving. Staying up-to-date is important for robot designers.

✔ Keep up with the latest AI developments at news sites like this one: https://www.wired.com/tag/robotics/.

Mechanical engineers design robots used to manufacture products in factories.

There are new robots being created all the time. Most of these new robots are designed by people with backgrounds in mechanical engineering.

Sometimes an engineer might create a robot that improves on older robot technology. In other cases, he or she might build a brand-new robot that is unlike anything ever seen before. In either case, any new project starts with a problem that needs to be solved. The engineer asks questions like "How can a robot walk up and down stairs faster?" or "Can we build a robot that makes pizzas as well as humans can?"

Engineers **brainstorm** ideas for answers to these questions. When they have a good idea for a robot, they build an early test version called a **prototype**. They test it and make more improvements. Each new version gets closer and closer to a finished product.

Future Mechanical Engineer

Robotics is a rapidly growing field, and it is likely to become even bigger in the future. If you want to get a job designing and building the latest robots, you'll probably need a college degree. You can also start learning about robotics right now. Many schools have robotics clubs for students to join. Club members build robots and compete against other robot creators!

Programmer

As you watch your family's robotic vacuum cleaner at work, you notice that it almost never makes mistakes. It avoids **obstacles** in the room and never bumps into walls. At the same time, it does a great job of sweeping up the entire floor. How did this little robot get so smart?

Think about a robot shaped like a person. It has arms, legs, and a head much like your own. It moves around a lot like you do. But inside, it is very different. It does not have a mind of its own, and it cannot think for itself. The closest thing it has to a brain is a computer that tells it what to do. But like all computers, the ones that control robots need instructions from their human creators before they can do anything. These instructions are called computer programs, or **software**.

Computer programs are not written in regular human languages. While some computers might be able to understand spoken English or other languages, it is only because a program tells them how! Instead, computer software is written in a number of different programming languages. There are many different programming languages, and new ones are always being created. Each one has its own purpose and most programmers are skilled at several of them.

Imagine It!

Imagine you're a programmer working on a robotic vacuum cleaner.

- Chart the list of steps the robot needs to follow to do its job.

- What order should the steps go in? Are there times the robot needs to choose between multiple possible steps? Should certain steps be repeated sometimes? Create branching paths in your chart.

- This is a lot like the process of writing a computer program.

Dig Deeper!

- Visit https://scratch.mit.edu to start learning the basics of computer programming.

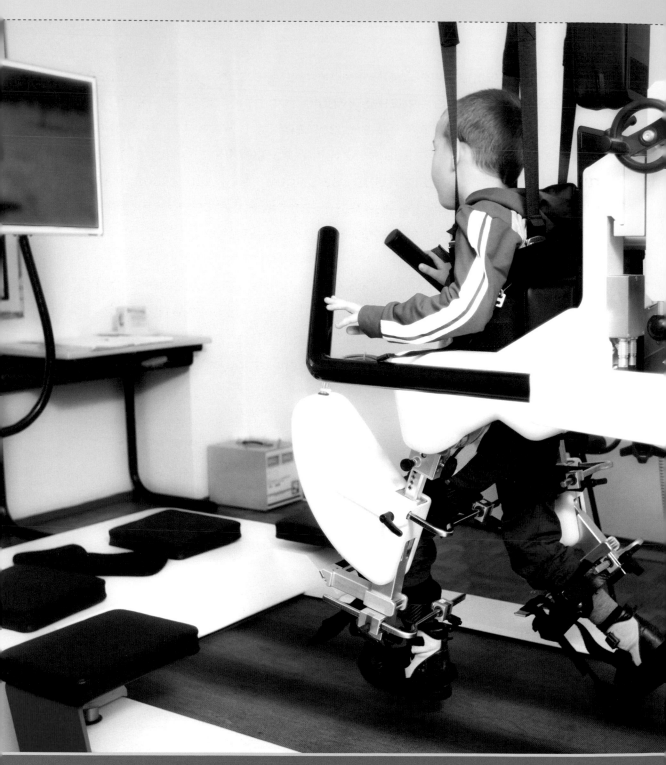

Some programmers write software for robots that help patients recover from injuries.

Programming languages combine words and phrases from human language with numbers, math symbols, and other characters. When and how these things should be used are determined by the rules of the programming language. It's like the spelling and grammar rules of the languages humans use to communicate. Lines of text written in a programming language are called code. Programmers can use code to make statements, ask questions, and more.

As they become experts in these languages, programmers learn to think like robots. They find new, efficient ways to write code that a robot's computer can read quickly. They come up with better, simpler ways to make robots perform complex tasks.

A robot depends on its programming to function. This means that any errors programmers make in their code can cause a robot to behave strangely or even stop working entirely. To prevent this, programmers spend a lot of time testing and revising their code until it is perfect.

Future Programmer

It is never too early to start learning how to write code. There are many online resources for learning the basics. All you need is a computer, smartphone, or tablet. Keep challenging yourself with more complex lessons, and don't be afraid to make mistakes. Practice makes perfect. Before long, writing code will come as naturally to you as speaking your native language!

Robot Technician

Many of today's factories depend on robots. If a robot on an **assembly line** breaks down, it can cause major problems. The factory will slow down or even stop, and the company might lose money. This means it is very important to keep the robots in tip-top condition!

Just like cars, dishwashers, and other items people use every day, robots are machines. They do not always work perfectly. As they are used, parts can wear out and need replacement. Accidents can leave robots broken and in need of repair. Improvements in technology can make useful **upgrades** available. When any of this work needs to be done, robot owners rely on skilled professionals called technicians.

Technicians are a lot like auto mechanics for robots. They are experts in the inner workings of a robot's machinery. When a robot **malfunctions**, a technician can examine the situation and start figuring out what caused the problem. He or she might use special tools to run tests on the robot. Once the problem is diagnosed, repairs can begin.

Mechanical issues aren't the only problems robots can run into. Most modern robots depend on computer software to function correctly. Like the programs on your school's computers, the software that powers a robot

Imagine It!

→ Next time you run into a computer problem or one of your toys breaks, try fixing it yourself.

→ Start by identifying the problem.

→ Think about possible solutions. Start with the simplest one and see if it works.

→ Ask an adult or search online if you need help.

Dig Deeper!

✓ Read interviews with National Aeronautics and Space Administration (NASA) robot experts to find out what they do at their jobs: http://bit.ly/RobotCareers.

✓ Pay close attention to the advice they offer students pursuing careers in robotics.

Technicians keep robotic systems running smoothly.

does not always work the way it is supposed to. Sometimes it might crash and stop working entirely. Other times it might cause a robot to act in unexpected ways. Just like when a robot needs repairs, technicians are called in to solve problems related to software.

Technicians are often responsible for upgrading robot software as manufacturers create new and improved versions. They might also perform regular tests on the robots to ensure they are functioning correctly. The earlier they can detect an issue, the fewer problems it will cause in the long run.

Some technicians might work full-time at factories and other places where there are many robots working all the time. Other technicians might be called in to job sites when people are having issues with their robots.

Future Robot Technician

Practice learning about what makes robots work by tinkering with robot-building kits such as Lego Mindstorms or Makeblock. As you build and program robots, you'll learn how to find mistakes and solve problems. Combined with a college degree in engineering or some other technical field, these skills will make you the perfect candidate for a robot technician job.

Robot Operator

With the tilt of a **joystick**, you send a robotic arm whirring off to the side. With a few button presses, you can use the arm to pick up huge, heavy pieces of metal and easily move them around. Can you imagine getting behind the controls of a high-tech robot? A job as a robot operator might be perfect for you!

Robots are able to do a lot of incredible things all on their own, without any help from people. The list of things robots can do is always increasing. This is what makes them so useful and why they are likely to be even more important in the future.

However, robots are still not perfect. As useful as they can be, they sometimes need help with certain tasks. Other times, they might simply need someone to keep an eye on them to make sure they aren't making mistakes. This is where robot operators come in.

Some robot operators directly control robots using joysticks, buttons, and other controls. It is a lot like driving a remote-controlled car or even playing a video game.

Sometimes a robot operator might be responsible for swapping out parts, tools, and materials on a robot to help it do its job. Or a robot might need to be cleaned from time to time as part of its normal operating process.

Imagine It!

- → There are many controllable toy robots available today.

- → Try driving Sphero (https://www.sphero.com) or Dash and Dot (https://www.makewonder.com). All you need is a tablet or smartphone and the robot.

- → If you don't have your own robot, ask your teachers. Many schools have robots for students to use.

Dig Deeper!

- ✓ Check out a state-of-the-art robot that operators can sit inside of and control with their arm movements: http://bit.ly/PopSciFi.

- ✓ Can you think of other ways people might control robots in the future?

Robot operators control robots used to manufacture products in factories.

This is especially common in factories where robots do most of the work of manufacturing products. Other basic **maintenance** duties might also be assigned to an operator.

At times, an operator might have to supply a robot with information for each specific job. For example, the robot might know that it needs to travel from place to place delivering objects. However, it needs to be told which path to follow.

Many robot operators learn skills on the job. In fact, becoming a robot operator is one of the few ways to work with robots without first earning a college degree. However, they must have a good understanding of technology.

Being able to work with and alongside robots will be an essential job skill for many people in the future. Robots are becoming more and more widespread in manufacturing, health care, and many other fields.

Future Robot Operator

Take every opportunity to play with robots or other machines. Driving a remote-controlled vehicle or flying a drone can also give you an idea of what to expect as a robot operator. A background in programming is always a good start if you want to work with robots. Depending on which kinds of robots you want to work with, you might need other technical skills as well.

Can You Imagine?

Innovation always starts with an idea. This was true for Alexander Graham Bell, Thomas Edison, Henry Ford, and the Wright brothers. It is still true today as innovators imagine new kinds of robots. And it will still be true in the future when you begin your high-tech career. So ...

What is your big idea?

Think of a cool way to use robots. Write a story or draw a picture to share your idea with others.

Please do **NOT** write in this book if it doesn't belong to you.
Gather your own paper and art supplies and get creative with your ideas!

Glossary

assembly line (uh-SEM-blee LINE) an arrangement of machines and workers in a factory, in which a product passes from one person or machine to another, with each performing a specific task, until the product is completely put together

brainstorm (BRAYN-storm) to think up ideas or solutions to a problem

components (kuhm-POH-nuhnts) parts of a machine

expertise (ek-spur-TEEZ) expert skill or knowledge about something

innovations (in-uh-VAY-shuhnz) new ideas or inventions

joystick (JOI-stik) a lever that can be moved in different directions to control a robot or computer game

maintenance (MAYN-tuh-nuhns) the process of keeping something in good condition by checking and repairing it

malfunctions (mal-FUNK-shuhnz) fails to work in a normal or efficient way

obstacles (AHB-stuh-kuhlz) things that make it difficult to go somewhere or get something done

prototype (PROH-tuh-tipe) the first version of an invention that tests an idea to see it if will work

robots (ROH-bahts) machines that are programmed to perform complex human tasks

skeleton (SKEL-uh-tuhn) the framework of bones that supports and protects the body of an animal with a backbone

software (SAWFT-wair) computer programs that control how a computer works and what it can do

upgrades (UHP-graydz) replacements of computer parts or software with better, more powerful, or newer versions

Index

About the Author

Joshua Gregory is the author of more than 125 books for young readers. He currently lives in Chicago, Illinois.